D0831367

LOVING THE HOLY MASS

$\mathcal{L}_{in}F$ ᴰᴱᶜ· 2014

LOVING THE HOLY MASS

❖

Edward G. Maristany

Scepter

The author is very thankful to Mary Gottschalk
for her indispensable help in editing this book.

First printing, March 2006
Second printing, March 2007
Third printing, October 2008
Fourth printing, November 2009
Fifth printing, February 2012

Copyright © 2006 Edward G. Maristany
Published by Scepter Publishers, Inc.,
P.O. Box 211, New York, NY 10018.
www.scepterpublishers.org

ISBN 1-59417-042-8
ISBN 978-1-59417-042-3

Printed in the United States of America

CONTENTS

INTRODUCTION

The priest had just finished his explanation about Mass. It was time for questions. A bright and well-educated Catholic high schooler asked the first one: "How late can a person arrive and still fulfill the precept of Sunday Mass?" The priest resented the question, but answered it. Then came the second question, and this one was too much for him: "How early can a person leave the Mass . . . ?" It felt like an unfair one–two punch, since he had been trying so hard to help them love the Mass.

And yet . . . how can I blame people who want to spend as little time as possible in church? I remember how, when I was a kid, we loved those midweek holidays when "you don't have to go to school, *and* you don't have to go to Mass."

Why did we cradle Catholics ever start going to Mass? Because we were told to. It was our duty. We didn't put up a lot of resistance, but perhaps neither did we put into it a lot of heart. How well many of us could relate ourselves to this real-life dialogue:

> *"Mom, what's the highest number you ever counted up to?"*
>
> *"Oh, I don't know, honey. What about you? What's your highest?"*
>
> *"Six thousand, one hundred and twelve."*
>
> *"Hmm. And why did you stop there?"*
>
> *"The Mass was over."*

And this one:

> *"Dad, why do you go to Mass on weekdays?"*
>
> *"Because I want to."*
>
> *"Well, why do you want to?"*
>
> *"Because I love going to Mass."*
>
> *"Oh. . . . Dad, I've got such a long way to go."*

Many adults are still going to Mass "because we have to," "because it's our duty." Not much has changed since their childhood. Maybe only that they now have a vague sense that "you do have to pay your dues," and that one hour a week is not an unreasonable price to pay God for one's life and all the blessings in it.

Some have offered negative reasons for going to Mass: "God wants us to worship him because he knows that the moment we stop worshiping him, we will start worshiping ourselves." "When people cease to believe in God, the problem is not that they believe in nothing; it's that they'll believe in anything."

Some have attempted to lure people to Mass by making it entertaining, by means of all kinds of theatrics.

Well, an adult Christian does not go to Mass because it is entertaining (it is not), or because it is inspiring and beautiful (it always is). An adult Christian goes to Mass because it is "the culmination both of God's action sanctifying the world in Christ and of the worship men offer to Christ and through him to the Father in the Holy Spirit." [1] We go to Mass because we want to *enter into communion with the Blessed Trinity, by uniting ourselves to the sacrifice of Jesus Christ and (when this is appropriate) partaking of his Body and Blood.*

The Eucharist is the memorial of Christ's Passover, the making present and the sacramental offering of his unique sacrifice, in the liturgy of the Church which is his Body.
—*Catechism of the Catholic Church*, no. 1362

JESUS' PLAN

We come to Mass to witness the most important event in human history, an occurrence that intimately affects every person. Saint Paul articulated that event in this way: "When the time had fully come, God sent forth his Son, born of woman, born under the law, to redeem those who were under the law, so that we might receive adoption as sons" (Gal 4:4–5).

God loves us so much that he became one of us, lived among us for thirty-three years doing nothing but good, offered himself up to a horrific passion and death, and rose back to life two days later. Thanks to all of that, we who were slaves can now be free; we who were condemned to death can now live eternally; we can be happy in this life and forever after. That is why we have history divided into two periods: before and after Christ. The Mass is for remembering, we being so prone to forget even the greatest gifts.

A mother explained that to her little daughter, and received the answer, "Yeah, but Mom, that all happened such a long time ago!"

Is that true? Well, yes and no. The Mass is not just a memorial of the Passion; it's not just for "remembering" in the usual sense of that word. Jesus himself, anticipating the natural reaction voiced by this little girl, made provision for much more.

The Eucharist "*re-presents* (makes present) the sacrifice of the cross": "it is its *memorial,*" and "it *applies* its fruit." [2] Thus "the sacrifice Christ offered once for all on the cross remains ever present," [3] an act of love for me that happened once and perdures through time.

The Mass is the way that Jesus came up with to make himself completely present to me and bring before my eyes—here and now—the sacrifice he offered for me on Calvary two thousand years ago. It is Jesus' way to renew—today—the offering he made of his body and blood on the cross for me. It is not just a memorial; it is the real thing.

For God, two thousand years is like a second. But it is not so for us, and so he knew that a *memorial*, in the usual sense of the word, would not have sufficed, because, having only that, we could always have excused ourselves by saying, "That all happened such a long time ago."

Think of this all-too-common exchange between a woman and her husband:

"You never tell me you love me."
"Well, I said it the day of our wedding, didn't I? I haven't changed my mind. What more do you want?"

God knows our every desire and need. The Mass is Jesus' way of reaffirming his "I do" every day. Of saying, "The sacrificial love that I showed on the cross is the same yesterday, today, and forever. It is here and now that I love you . . . to death."

At the high point of every Mass, we hear these words: "This is the cup of my blood, the blood of the new and everlasting covenant." Let us for a moment reflect on this: a covenant that is new *and* everlasting. Isn't that what we all long for—a love both fresh and stable, exciting and secure?

The night before his death, Jesus composed his last will and testament, and executed it. He, who had nothing else, bequeathed the only thing he could bequeath: his own self. He gathered his immediate beneficiaries—all twelve of them— and gave them the Eucharist, making them priests with the power to consecrate bread and wine so that they would become his body and blood. Through priests, (*a*) his upcoming *sacrifice* on the cross would be made present for us through time and space; (*b*) he himself would remain really and truly *present* to us under the appearances of bread and wine; (*c*) we would be able to have the most intimate and intense sacramental union with him, by receiving his body and blood in *Communion*.

Sacrifice. Presence. Communion. Let us see how in these three ways Jesus stays actively present among us, in every place and every age.

The Eucharist is above all else a sacrifice.
—Pope John Paul II, *Dominicae Cenae*, no. 9

1. A SACRIFICE

To understand and appreciate the Mass, and to benefit from it, one first has to understand and appreciate Jesus' sacrifice on the cross. Why did he do it?

For the very same reason that he became "Jesus" to start with. The Son of God came into the human race to free it from the choke hold that sin had on it. Sin is the only true evil in the universe, and he conquered it.

We humans are the only creatures on earth that are made free and thus capable of rejecting the Creator. And reject him we do, from the dawn of history to the present day. What could be done to remedy this terrible situation?

Well, couldn't God have just dropped the charges? Couldn't he have ignored all our sins? Surely we mere humans, on this tiny planet, can't be so important to the God of the universe that he could seriously be concerned about our foibles!

That's precisely the point.

The ceaselessly surprising answer is: Yes, we can be and are important to him. As Saint Thomas Aquinas explains, God could indeed have chosen to free us from the bondage of sin without any satisfaction being made by anyone.[4] But had he done that, had he just shrugged off all our sins, that would have been like saying, "What you puny little creatures do means nothing to me," which would equate to, "*You* mean nothing to me."

It is precisely because we mean so much to him that he went drastically out of his way to help us.

To help us in the way that he saw fit to, the first thing he needed to do was to open our eyes to the seriousness of sin. Leviticus, the third book of the Bible, is all about sacrifices, purifications, priesthood, etc. One obsessive concern runs throughout: "What do we do with sin?" Sin happens . . . and I cannot take it back. It is, in fact, the great concern that has tormented humanity all along.

In Leviticus, God arranges a provisional solution: he instructs his people to offer certain sacrifices for their personal sins. These sacrifices typically consist in the slaughtering of an animal, like a lamb or a goat, and are offered on an ad hoc basis. And then, once a year, on the Day of Atonement, the high priest "shall lay both his hands upon the head of the live goat, and confess over him all the iniquities of the people of Israel, and all their transgressions, all their sins; and he shall put them upon the head of the goat, and send him away into the wilderness by the hand of a man who is in readiness. The goat shall bear all their iniquities upon him to a solitary land" (Lev 16: 21–22). This is where the word "scapegoat" comes from.

In the Old Testament, sin is presented as the revolt and ingratitude of a favored child against the most loving of fathers. But that favored child was not an individual, but a collectivity: Israel.

In the New Testament, Jesus completes the explanation of the meaning of sin by making it *personal*. Sin is shown to be essentially *a personal filial offense*. An offense not against a "Creator," but against a Father. And a Father who, in his infinite goodness and mercy, is willing to do whatever it takes to move his wayward child to reconciliation.

But how do you move to reconciliation someone who is unaware of the seriousness of what they have done?

The answer came to a friend of mine years ago, by means of a painful experience. On a Friday evening a colleague called him at home and proceeded to insult him with much colorful profanity, pointing out his defects and cursing him . . . and then hanging up, before he could say a word in response. In different circumstances, one might be able to let something like this slide, but my friend was in the delicate situation that, on the following Monday, the two of them would have to be working together. He was willing to forgive the man, but how can you offer forgiveness to someone who does not want to be forgiven, who is not offering you an apology? Facing this impasse, my friend resorted to prayer, saying, "Lord, what can I do?" And it took him all of two seconds to hear the answer: "Do what I did."

What did God do when we offended him? He sent a mediator: his Son. My friend needed a mediator. So he called up another colleague, told him what had transpired, and said, "Would you be willing to talk to him and make him see that he has wronged me and that he should apologize to me? On my part, I am willing to put all this behind us." "I'll try," he promised. A few minutes later he called back, saying, "I've just spoken with him. He is sorry, and will apologize." And the following Monday, as soon as he got to work, this man came to my friend with a sincere apology, and that was the end of it. My friend says that from that moment on, they never again had any major conflicts.

Of course, being a trinity of persons, God did not have to reach outside of himself to find a mediator. God the Son took on that role: "For there is one God. There is also one mediator between God and man, the man Christ Jesus, who gave himself as ransom for all" (1 Tim 2:5).

Why is the cross the sign of the Christian? Because on a cross God died for us; that was the price God paid for our sins.

And so, when I look at a crucifix—Jesus hanging on a cross—it *helps me understand* the seriousness of sin, of my sins.[5]

Sometimes I hear the dramatic expression, "It was my sins that nailed Jesus to the cross." This is more than a metaphor. Its proper meaning is, "My sins made it necessary for the Word of God to become flesh and undergo his Passion and death. My sins made me so thickheaded that only in the sight of Jesus on the cross could I *open my eyes* to the seriousness of my faults and begin to understand how much my heavenly Father cares when I mess up."

Suppose God came up and asked you, "What do I need to do to prove that I really love you?" The rest of that conversation would probably go something like this, right? "Well, Lord, let's keep it simple. Give me a million bucks and I'll consider it proved." "Okay."

Now suppose it happened. Would he have actually proved his love for you? Let's be honest. We both know it cost him nothing to give you that money. He zapped it up out of nowhere, out of *nothing*, and could always zap up billions more, anytime.

Then you'd have to say, "All right, Lord, I lied. The only way we humans believe that something is true love is if this is proved by sacrifice. It has to cost us. The more it costs us, the truer that love is proved to be."

And so, God the Father gave us the only "thing" that he (by himself[6]) had in short supply, as Jesus discreetly intimates in this line from one of his parables: "He still had one other, a beloved son; finally he sent him to them" (Mk 12: 6).

God the Son became a man and offered himself up to death because "greater love has no man than this, that a man lay down his life for his friends" (Jn 15: 13). He made the ultimate sacrifice, the one that proves beyond any reasonable doubt God's unconditional love for us.

The old question "What do we do with sin?" has now received its definitive answer. The sacrifice of Christ has replaced all of the Old Testament sacrifices. Jesus is now the only victim. He is also the high priest, offering himself as the definitive scapegoat. John the Baptist pointed this out when he said, "Behold, the Lamb of God, who takes away the sin of the world!" (Jn 1: 29).

The Mass is not a re-presentation of the Last Supper. And neither is it in every way identical to the sacrifice of the cross. The Mass is *in its essence* the sacrifice of the cross, brought about *in the manner of* the Last Supper.

In Eucharistic Prayer I (also known as the Roman Canon), the priest invokes three characters from the Old Testament. He prays: "Look with favor on these offerings and accept them as once you accepted the gifts of your servant Abel, the sacrifice of Abraham, our father in faith, and the bread and wine offered by your priest Melchisedech." [7]

Why, of all the great figures of the Old Testament, does the Church mention those three? Why not Noah, Isaac, and Jacob, or Moses and David, or Esther, Rebecca, and Ruth?

The three were chosen for their symbolic relevance:

• Abel offered to God in sacrifice the best of his flock. His offerings represent all the bloody sacrifices of the Old Testament.

• Abraham, by his willingness to obey God's command to sacrifice his beloved son Isaac, did in such a real way make that sacrifice that it became the figure of the only New Testament one, which is *in essence* the sacrifice of the Son of God on the cross.

• The bread and wine offered by the priest Melchisedech are a figure of the *manner* in which the new sacrifice will be offered by Christ's priests until the end of time.

Now—let's review: Why do we go to Mass? Primarily, to enter into communion with the Blessed Trinity through the sacrifice of Jesus Christ. And how do we do this? By offering ourselves with Jesus to the Father in the Holy Mass. Jesus is the scapegoat, and when we unite ourselves with him, we enter into communion with the God who forgives us and blesses us. The Mass is the great transformer; it turns everything we bring to it into an offering of gratitude pleasing to God.

"Jesus," says a saint of our times, "reminds all of us: 'And I, if I be lifted up from the earth, I will draw all things to myself ' (Jn 12:32). If you put me at the center of all earthly activities, he is saying, by fulfilling the duty of each moment, in what appears important and what appears unimportant, I will draw everything to myself. My kingdom among you will be a reality!" [8]

Well—what do we do with sin now? Do we get rid of it just by this one step of going to Mass? No. Spiritual life is rich, and it is multi-dimensional—as is physical or intellectual or emotional life. The Church says, Avail yourselves of this other wonderful sacrament: the sacrament of Reconciliation, instituted by Jesus for the very purpose of cleansing you from sin. And there we go, with contrite heart, and dump on the priest (Christ's representative) all our sins—plus, very often, a number of other things that make us suffer. And the priest, often after giving us some helpful advice, gives us absolution, and then we go home relieved and thankful.

I know good priests who spend many hours in the confessional every day; they feel specially called to do for God this "spiritual laundering." In fact, the patron saint of parish priests is Saint John Vianney (the Curé of Ars), who often spent sixteen to eighteen hours a day seated in the confessional box.

What does a priest do with all that gets dumped on him there? Let it roll off his back? A doctor, a counselor, or an advice columnist can "leave it at the office," but a priest cannot. To be a priest is to let those sins get to you, weigh on you. To be a priest is to have a heart that bleeds for the miseries of souls, and for what God has to endure as well. What does the priest do with this terrible burden? The only thing he can do: he staggers up to the altar of sacrifice, extends his two hands over the offerings, and passes it on. This is the great, cosmic "passing of the buck," upon the Lamb of God. Through the Mass, that burden will rise to heaven as incense does, giving off a pleasant aroma, because Jesus, the scapegoat, takes away those sins and transforms them into good.

It's a dream come true: that of the philosopher's stone, which changes ordinary materials into gold. Or, to relate it to a reality rather than a myth, it's like the business of producing electrical energy out of the garbage we humans produce. "From trash to cash," as the saying goes.

Without the holy sacrifice of the Mass, the priest would not be able to survive. It is that simple. This is the big difference between a "minister" and a priest. It is also the connection between the sacraments of Reconciliation and the Eucharist. You hear the words of the absolution in the confessional. But the power to forgive sins comes from the Holy Mass. As Scripture says, "Without the shedding of blood there is no forgiveness of sins" (Heb 9: 22).

That is what the priest brings to Mass in the exercise of his *ministerial priesthood*.

But all of the faithful—including the priest—enjoy a *common priesthood* received through the sacrament of Baptism. "In the Eucharist the sacrifice of Christ becomes also the sacrifice of the members of his Body. The lives of the faithful, their praise, sufferings, prayer, and work, are united with those of Christ and with his total offering, and so acquire a new value." [9]

What do we bring to the Mass? What are we dragging to the altar? What is it that we feel the need to bring into the presence of the Lord?

Ultimately, those love the Mass who recognize their need of the Mass.

—*Who Needs the Mass?*

Those need the Mass who know how to love. These are the people who have a big heart, because they have rid themselves of the shackles of self-interest, have lost the fear of suffering for others, and have taken upon themselves the pain of others, sharing their burdens.

Those also need the Mass who are painfully aware that they do not know how to love. This category includes those who are distressed by their coldness, their self-centeredness, their repugnance toward having to deal with other people's problems. Those who desperately want a heart of flesh, and recognize all too well that they are never going to get one on their own.

John's account concerning the night when Jesus instituted the Eucharist begins with this sentence: "Now before the feast of the Passover, when Jesus knew that his hour had come to depart out of this world to the Father, having loved his own who were in the world, he loved them to the end" (Jn 13: 1). Here, "to the end"

means "to the max." Jesus proceeded to antici-
pate *sacramentally* his sacrificial death, and
then march toward Calvary. He was in effect
saying, "Let's roll. Let me complete my mission.
Bring on the cross."

For someone who loves, or very much wants
to love—and who, either way, therefore suf-
fers—the Mass *hits the spot*.

Think: What burdens do I carry in my heart?
What do I bring with me?

> *I bring you, Lord, first of all, the weight of
> my sins, my infidelities, my omissions, my
> ingratitude, my self-centeredness. I bring you
> the nothing, or the worse than nothing, that
> I am.*

> *I bring you, Lord, my concerns for my family,
> particularly Uncle Joe, who recently had a
> stroke, and my son Jason, who doesn't go to
> Mass anymore, and my third daughter, Susie,
> who is going out with that older, twice-
> married guy.*

Where else can I go with my sorrows? Whom
can I entrust them to? Whom else could I go to
and say, "Here—there's nothing else I can do for
these people—you take care of them"? That's
what we go to Mass for: to pass the buck.

Of course, while we are passing those bucks,
we are also handing over our own selves.
"Come to me, all who labor and are heavy

laden, and I will give you rest. Take my yoke upon you, and learn from me; for I am gentle and lowly in heart, and you will find rest for your souls. For my yoke is easy, and my burden is light" (Mt 11: 28-30). We may well find, by taking the Lord up on that invitation, that there is something we could say or do to alleviate at least some of these overwhelming situations that we are bringing to him.

Lord, I bring you my financial worries. I bring you the exam that my son Jimmy is having today. I bring you the troubles I'm having with my boss. I bring you the difficulties that my coworker Peter is having in his marriage.

I bring you, Lord, my concern for my husband, who is working too many hours. I bring you the preparations for our anniversary next week. And I bring you my good friend Cathy, who is scared because she is pregnant at age forty-four.

I bring you, Lord, my concerns for my country. I bring you my desire for good elected officials. I bring you my worries about laws that are injurious to marriage, the family, human life, or the education of children.

I bring you, Lord, all those who have been so good and generous to me— all those people I will never be able to thank enough. I bring you all the intentions I have been asked to pray for. I bring you the troubles of everyone: "prisoners, orphans, pilgrims, the weak, the sick, the old, the young, the virgins, the widows." [10]

We could go on forever. There is absolutely nothing in the Mass for someone who is and wants to remain an uncaring, self-absorbed, mind-my-own-business type of person, who thinks in terms of "boundaries" and shuns involvement in other people's "issues." But for a soul bent on living a life of love, the Mass is the only thing that fits the bill.

In his *Confessions*—an autobiography, written more than fifteen centuries ago, that reads like new and has continuously been in print in all major languages—Saint Augustine recalls that when his brother told their failing mother, (Saint) Monica, of their hope that she would live long enough to make it back to her homeland and be buried there, she replied, "It doesn't matter where you bury my body. Don't let that worry you! All I ask of you is that, wherever you may be, you remember me at the altar of the Lord." [11] She well knew where the power is, she who for so long had begged before the altar of God for the conversion of that now-famous son of hers.

The Mass is Christ offering to God the Father the perfect gift of his own infinite love. Not his own love alone; he unites with it yours and mine. He gathers up whatever love is to be found in the hearts of the members of his Mystical Body, and he integrates it into his love. The Holy Mass is, therefore, a *corporate* act of worship. It is the whole Body that offers the Mass. Christ made the gift of his love once on the cross—once and for all. But his death is not just a historical fact, something that happened some two thousand years ago. In a sense, Christ, on the cross, hangs before God the Father forever. The sacrifice of the Mass is the means by which Christ reaches down through time, to collect the love of our hearts, which he pledged to the Father on Calvary.[12]

*Under the consecrated species of bread and
wine Christ himself, living and glorious,
is present in a true, real, and substantial
manner: his Body and his Blood, with his soul
and his divinity (cf. Council of Trent:
DS 1640; 1651).*

—*Catechism of the Catholic Church*, no. 1413

---

2. A REAL PRESENCE

A contemporary saint presents a very simple
and moving explanation of the Eucharistic
presence:

*Think of the human experience of two people
who love each other, and yet are forced to
part. They would like to stay together forever,
but duty—in one form or another—forces
them to separate. They are unable to fulfill
their desire of remaining close to each other,
so man's love—which, great as it may be, is
limited—seeks a symbolic gesture. People who
make their farewells exchange gifts or perhaps a photograph with a dedication so ar-
dent that it seems almost enough to burn that
piece of paper. They can do no more, because
a creature's power is not so great as its desire.*

*What we cannot do, our Lord is able to do.
Jesus Christ, perfect God and perfect man,
leaves us, not a symbol, but a reality. He
himself stays with us. He will go to the Father,*

but he will also remain among men. He will leave us, not simply a gift that will make us remember him, not an image that becomes blurred with time, like a photograph that soon fades and yellows, and has no meaning except for those who were contemporaries. Under the appearances of bread and wine, he is really present, with his body and blood, with his soul and divinity.[13]

In a no less personalist fashion, Monsignor Ronald Knox completes the idea:

The whole fullness of the Godhead dwelt in human form; dwelt for a time in the form of a little baby on his mother's breast. The God who made all things and upholds all things by the word of his power became part of his own creation, as it were, confined himself within the conditions of time and space, for our sakes, so as to be closer to us.

But, you see, that wasn't enough for him. If he was to live the life of an ordinary man, that life must come to an end; his presence on earth would be limited to a particular period of human history, and those who were born, like ourselves, long after that period would no longer be able to say to one another, "Jesus of Nazareth passes by."

And again, a human body, like any other natural object, is present at one single point in space, and is absent from all other points in space; if our Lord were living now, as Man, in Palestine, only those of us who are rich enough to afford the journey to Palestine would be able to go and see him.

So he determined at once to perpetuate and to universalize the miracle of his Incarnation by the miracle of the Holy Eucharist. It had got to be possible for us, living nineteen centuries after the time of the Emperor Tiberius, living far away from Palestine, at the other end of the next continent, to say, "Here is Christ! Here is the human Body of Jesus of Nazareth present in our midst!" That is what the Blessed Sacrament makes possible.[14]

Do you find the Real Presence hard to believe in, or to appreciate, because you can't feel it or in any way perceive it? Here is a reflection that may be of some help. If you were to walk into a room saturated with radiation, you wouldn't see, hear, or smell anything unusual. But, given enough time, it would kill you. Similarly, Jesus' presence in the Eucharist cannot be perceived by your senses, but intense, frequent, unobstructed exposure to it will make you thrive. "Unobstructed exposure" meaning that you are not in some way blocking his life-giving presence—by, for instance, being in the state of mortal sin or in deliberate distractedness.

Here I would like also to encourage devotion to the Blessed Sacrament, by passing on to you a true story that I find deeply moving:

A couple of months before his death, Bishop Fulton J. Sheen was interviewed on national television. One of the questions was this: "Bishop Sheen, you have inspired millions of people all over the world. Who inspired you?"

Bishop Sheen responded that it was not a pope, a cardinal, another bishop, or even a priest or a nun. It was a little Chinese girl of eleven years of age. He explained that when the Communists took over China, they imprisoned a priest in his own rectory near the church. After they locked him up in his own house, the priest was horrified to look out the window and see the Communists proceed into the church, where they went into the sanctuary and broke into the tabernacle. In an act of hateful desecration, they took the ciborium and threw it on the floor, with all of the sacred hosts spilling out. The priest knew exactly how many hosts were in the ciborium: thirty-two.

When the Communists left, they either did not notice or didn't pay any attention to a small girl praying in the back of the church who saw everything that had happened. That night the little girl came back. Slipping past the guard at the priest's house, she went inside the church. There she made a holy hour of prayer, an act of love to make up for the act of hatred.

After her holy hour she went into the sanctuary, knelt down, bent over, and with her tongue received Jesus in Holy Communion, since it was not permissible at that time for lay people to touch the sacred host with their hands.

The little girl continued to come back each night to make her holy hour and receive Jesus in Holy Communion on her tongue. On the thirty-second night, after she had consumed the last host, the thirty-second one, she accidentally made a noise and woke the guard, who was sleeping. He ran after her, caught her, and beat her to death with the butt of his rifle.

This act of heroic martyrdom was witnessed by the priest as he watched grief-stricken from his bedroom window.

When Bishop Sheen heard the story, he was so inspired that he promised God he would make a holy hour of prayer before the Blessed Sacrament every day of his life.[15]

Not only did Bishop Sheen keep that promise, but he often said that this daily devotion was the secret to his great success in touching hearts and winning souls for Christ.

3. A MEAL (HOLY COMMUNION)

Jesus was not content just to stay with us, totally accessible, more vulnerable even than in the manger or on the cross. He longed for an even more intimate union with us.

—*In Communion with Jesus' Body and Blood*

Our present cultural environment does, from one point of view, make it difficult to be enthusiastic about the way that Jesus makes himself totally present to us. In a world where our attention is constantly being clamored and competed for (on billboards, on TV, on the radio, on the Net, and even on the phone), Jesus seems to have no idea of how to compete. Where is the zing? Where is the hook? We are constantly being encouraged to fulfill ourselves, and to stand out as interesting and powerful individuals . . . and here is Jesus, in the guise of jillions of identical almost nothings: small, round, white, thin pieces of unleavened bread. How can he hope to get anyone's attention in that way?

But precisely in that way, he *does* prove to be the most distinctive, powerful, interesting person that ever walked the face of the earth. Who else ever aspired to be people's *food*? We, who pride ourselves on being "at the top of the food chain," are struck speechless by this God whose idea of the "good life" is to set foot into the human race as one human among others; then show the depths of his love for us by suffering for our sakes torture, ridicule, and execution as a criminal; and finally, after rising from the dead, stay with us throughout our time on earth, as our food.

When we say of someone, "He thinks he's God," what do we mean? We mean he is arrogant, overbearing, full of himself, forever demanding that others cater to him. But the one human being who really is God is so radically the opposite—so humble, so unostentatious, so focused on giving himself to fulfill others—that he is by far the most captivating. "The humility of Jesus: in Bethlehem, in Nazareth, on Calvary. But still more humiliation and more self-abasement in the most sacred host—more than in the stable, more than in Nazareth, more than on the

38

cross. That is why I must love the Mass so! (*Our Mass, Jesus.*)" [16]

He knew, from his own experience, that a human being is not only a soul, or mostly a soul, or a soul imprisoned in a body. Jesus' body, with its particular characteristics and faculties, was as integral to his humanity as was his soul. That is why he ascended into heaven with his body and with his soul, and why we can say, in the present, that he continues to be a perfect man.

He also knew that it is of the perfection of human love to care for the full humanity of the other, not merely for his or her soul or spiritual qualities. He loves us perfectly: our souls and our bodies. Consequently, he longed to unite himself to us also in body and soul.

And so, he gave us his flesh.

First he promised it, saying, "I am the living bread which came down from heaven; if any one eats of this bread, he will live for ever. . . . Truly, truly, I say to you, unless you eat the flesh of the Son of man and drink his blood, you have no life in you; he who eats my flesh and drinks my blood has eternal life, and I will raise him up at the last day. For my flesh is food indeed, and my blood is drink indeed. He who eats my flesh and drinks my blood abides in me, and I in him. As the living Father sent me, and I live because of the Father, so he who eats me will live because of me" (Jn 6: 51–57).

And the night before his Passion, he carried out that promise. "Jesus took bread and blessed and broke it, and gave it to the disciples and said, 'Take, eat; this is my body.' And he took a cup, and when he had given thanks he gave it to them, saying, 'Drink of it, all of you; for this is my blood of the new covenant . . .' " (Mt 26: 26–28).

"Think for a moment," says Monsignor Knox, "what it would be like . . . if we Christian people had all the other opportunities of worship to which we are accustomed, the Mass, and the Blessed Sacrament in the tabernacle, and Benediction, and processions of the Blessed Sacrament, but there were no such thing as receiving holy Communion. . . . We should still be able to say, with a prouder boast than the Jews of old, 'See how close our God comes to us.' But he wanted us to be able to say something better. . . . He wanted us to be able to say, 'See how close my God comes to me.' " [17]

I need to know not only whether God loves *us*, but whether he loves *me*. It is good to know that God cares about people's affairs. But I need to believe that he cares about *my* affairs.

The baby in the crib of Bethlehem and the man on the cross of Calvary are the proofs of the former; Jesus in Holy Communion is the proof of the latter. He loves me and cares for me, so he comes and unites himself to me.

Those two vital dimensions—the specific and the general, the personal and the communal—are simply and beautifully reflected in the words "for you and for all," in the formula for the consecration of the wine.

—Who May Receive Communion?

If Communion is that vital—if it is true that "unless you eat the flesh of the Son of man and drink his blood, you have no life in you"—then why are any restrictions placed as to who may receive it? In particular: Why exclude non-Catholics, or non-Christians? Doesn't everyone need Jesus, regardless?

Why exclude those in the state of mortal sin? Don't they need Communion the most?

The key to the answer is in the very word "communion." Communion is not a one-way street. What Jesus could do unilaterally, he did. By his incarnation he became a brother to us all, and by his Passion and death he won redemption for us all. But communion is something that cannot be accomplished only by him or any other one person; it takes two wills to make it possible.

In Holy Communion, Jesus surrenders his entire self—Body and Blood, soul and divinity—to *me*. If I in my mind and heart do not entirely accept him, or if I am in a state of alienation from him on account of unabsolved mortal sin, then my "communion" is really no such thing.

Why exclude non-Catholics, or even non-Christians? Because Jesus' entire self includes the Church. The Church is Christ's mystical body. As Saint Paul writes: "The husband is the head of the wife as Christ is the head of the church, his body. . . . No man ever hates his own flesh, but nourishes and cherishes it, as Christ does the church, because we are members of his body" (Eph 5: 23, 29). Christ's Body is part and parcel with the Church.

When we say with body language something that is at variance with what is in our minds and hearts, we are not being honest. If I totally receive Jesus with and into my body, but in my mind and heart I am traveling in a different orbit, then "Houston, we have a problem." Being separated from the Church that he founded does constitute a serious divergence. That is not to say that non-Catholics are bad people or that they cannot go to heaven. It is only to recognize that they, often through no fault of their own, are not in full union with Jesus' Body in its ecclesial dimension, and therefore it is generally not appropriate for them to receive Communion.[18]

Why exclude those in the state of mortal sin? Because to receive Communion while being spiritually separated from God, is not only dishonest but also insulting.

Mortal sin is a grave offense against God that turns our hearts away from him and necessarily kills the relationship of love that once existed between us.[19] Receiving Communion in that state would be a horrible abuse, like pouring salt on the wound.

To offset the damage caused by mortal sin, mumbling some offhand apology is not enough. There needs to be an explicit acknowledgment of the offense, a vocal begging of forgiveness, a firm resolution not to repeat the sin, and an outward expression of repentance and love,

However, in the case of a minor offense, a simple "Sorry" might do, and receiving Holy Communion with the right intention may very well heal the wound. It may even make one less likely to commit a major offense.

Receiving Holy Communion is proper only as an act of complete and mutual self-giving, with no reservation or obstruction. It is authentic only if it is the expression of a total, unqualified union that has already been solemnly, verbally established (by baptism or a profession of faith) and is not currently obstructed by a serious offense.

These, then, are the sensibilities behind the Church's teachings about who may receive Holy Communion: "The Eucharist is properly the sacrament of those who are in full communion with the Church"; "The Eucharist strengthens our charity, . . . and this loving charity wipes away venial sins"; "By the same charity that it enkindles in us, the Eucharist preserves us from future mortal sins"; "Anyone aware of having sinned mortally must not receive communion without having received absolution in the sacrament of penance."[20]

It is not sufficient to desire to be on good terms with Jesus, or to wish to unite oneself with him, or to feel the need for receiving him; one must be in full union with his Body the Church, and in the state of grace.

—Who Needs Communion?

Who needs communion with the Body and Blood of Christ? Anyone suffering like the Israelites who endured slavery in Egypt. God instructed them how to carry out the Passover meal. They were to kill a young unblemished lamb; mark the entrances to their homes with its blood, so that God's angel would "pass over" those houses, sparing them from death; and eat the lamb that had been sacrificed (see Exodus 12). This is the most precious prefigurement of the Eucharist.

Who needs communion with the Body and Blood of Christ? Anyone suffering like the prophet Elijah, who had to run for his life from the rage of Queen Jezebel after the great drought. Finally, unable to take it anymore, he prayed, "Lord, take away my life; for I am no better than my fathers" (1 Kings 19: 4). But the answer he got was that he should get up and eat, lest the journey be too long for him. "And he arose, and ate and drank, and went in the strength of that food forty days and forty nights to Horeb, the mountain of God." This, too, is a prefigurement of the Eucharist.

Who needs communion with the Body and Blood of Christ? Anyone longing for more faith and hope, as were those two travelers who met up with the risen Jesus on their way home to Emmaus. Their hopes had been shattered by his horrible death. Now, along the way, he prepared them with the "liturgy" of his word, and then, once invited into their home, he restored their faith and hope with the "liturgy" of the breaking of the bread. (See Luke 24: 13–35.)

Who needs communion with the Body and Blood of Christ? Anyone experiencing the sorrows and joys spoken of in the Beatitudes, concerning the poor in spirit, the meek, those who mourn, those who hunger for justice, those who practice mercy, those who are clean of heart, those who are persecuted because of righteousness. Anyone who can truthfully say to the Lord, "As a hart longs for flowing streams, so longs my soul for you, O God. My soul thirsts for God, for the living God. When shall I come and behold the face of God?" (Ps 42: 1–2).

This sacrifice is so decisive for the salvation of the human race that Jesus Christ offered it and returned to the Father only after he had left us a means of sharing in it as if we had been present there. Each member of the faithful can thus take part in it and inexhaustibly gain its fruits.

—Pope John Paul II, *Ecclesia de Eucharistia*, no. 11

HOW TO LIVE AND LOVE
THE MASS

"But I don't like that priest. I don't like his sermons. . . ." "I don't like the music. . . ." "I don't like this church. . . ."

All right, can we talk? I know that for many of you, the externals of the Masses in your parish can be so off-putting, so not conducive to prayer, as to make you feel it couldn't hurt to skip Sunday Mass at least occasionally, since you get practically nothing out of it anyway, whereas out in God's beautiful world of nature—away from that dreadful so-called music, or those lifeless homilies, or that too stuffy or too perky atmosphere—you can really feel his presence and pray.

It would be great if the externals all helped you to feel God's presence and to pray. I wish they did; and I and many, many of my fellow priests do all that we can toward making that be the case. But, as the saying goes, "You can please all of the people some of the time, and some of the people all of the time, but not all of the people all of the time." The thing is, the Eucharist is Christ's sacrifice offered not only by himself, but also by the *Church*, and the Church is made up of people with different (and often clashing) temperaments, tastes, sensibilities. And "people" includes priests.

The truth is that you probably would, at least on occasion, find it easier on your nerves to just skip Mass and pray on your own instead. *But*, is that what the Lord wants you to do? Which is really more worthwhile—to go to Sunday Mass, even though it may be impossible for you to feel close to God there, or (instead) to pray to him on your own in a setting where you almost certainly will feel close to him?

We are being called upon to witness, and to share in, Christ's *sacrifice*. When Jesus made that sacrifice on Calvary, he did not feel good. He lost all feeling of closeness to God. He cried out in agony, "My God, my God, why have you forsaken me?" How can you rightly be willing to be present at the reenactment of that sacrifice, and to participate in it, only in circumstances that are comfortable for you?

Maybe you're not comfortable unless the music is very lofty—or very down-to-earth. Maybe you are irked by efforts to "degenderize" the language—or by the lack of them. But really, so what? When the music or the language hurts our sensibilities, let's think for a moment how dreadful the original soundtrack must have been!

We come to Mass to thank God for and participate in the agonizingly painful sacrifice by which the Lord redeemed us. Discomforts, therefore, should be viewed not as detriments that we can use as excuses, but as pains that we can lovingly unite to those that the Lord suffered for us. And they should not be allowed to obscure our view of the big picture. Listen to what a great father of the Church said:

> *You cannot pray at home as at church, where there is a great multitude, where exclamations are cried out to God as from one great heart, and where there is something more: the union of minds, the accord of souls, the bond of charity, the prayers of the priests.*[21]

Now, here are a few ideas that may help you enter into this mystery of faith and communion with the Trinity, this mystery which is *your* Mass.

1. *Your Preparation for the Mass*
You need to get to Mass early. Aim always at being seated with at least five minutes to go.

Use that time to get into the scene, and into the character in it that you are.

Ask yourself: What is going to happen here? And what is my contribution? What am I bringing? What is in my heart these days?

Take this opportunity to improve your relationship with God. Thank him, praise him, apologize to him, ask him, for something in particular. Offer yourself to him without conditions, and try to enter into the flow of his love.

2. *Introductory Rites* [22]

The first part of the Mass is marked by its penitential character. We want to ask for forgiveness, to tune up to the Love that is being offered to us. You confess to God and "to you, my brothers and sisters," that you have sinned in thought, word, deed, and lack of deed; you beg the Blessed Virgin Mary, all the angels and saints, and "you, my brothers and sisters," to "pray for me to the Lord our God"; and then you do this praying, saying, "Lord, have mercy. Christ, have mercy. Lord, have mercy." As you can see, you make the act of contrition with the entire congregation, but it is for your own personal sins that you are to express sincere sorrow.

This part concludes with the Opening Prayer (also called the Collect). The priest announces it ("Let us pray") and pauses. Now is the moment to make your more important intention present to your mind. Then the priest opens his arms, "collects" the prayers of all the faithful, and presents them to God in the form of the Opening Prayer. He directs them to the Father, through the Son, in union with the Holy Spirit.

3. *The Liturgy of the Word*

Did you know that if you were to go to Mass every day, you would hear practically the entire Bible proclaimed from the lectern every three years? And, of course, some sections many more times.

These texts are God's word, and God's word is never old news. "For the word of God is living and active, sharper than any two-edged sword, piercing to the division of soul and spirit, of joints and marrow, and discerning the thoughts and reflections of the heart" (Heb 4:12). Listen to the proclamation of the word. The readers, it is true, are fallible human beings like us, and sometimes they are not very helpful—you cannot understand what they say, or you are distracted by their outfits or mannerisms, or they are declaiming rather than proclaiming. Listen to them, but don't feel obliged to do only that. Avail yourself of one of those missalettes that practically every parish church has in its pews. Or, better yet, bring your own missal. For getting focused, avoiding distraction, and absorbing what is said, two senses are better than one. That is true even when the reader is good.

Listen to the sermon and apply it to yourself, not your neighbor. Ask God what it is that he would like you to do—it doesn't necessarily have to be what the priest is suggesting—and bring this, too, to the altar.

4. *Preparation of the Altar and of the Gifts*

This is also the time to present your offering. The money you put in the collection basket is just part of it. Think about your life: this day, this week, the one just past, and the one to come. Turn it all over to Jesus. Put yourself on the altar, to be transformed into him. Say to him, "My Lord and my God, into your hands I abandon the past and the present and the future, what is small and what is great, what amounts to a little and what amounts to a lot, things temporal and things eternal." [23]

5. *The Eucharistic Prayer*

This is the climax of the liturgy. The priest alone speaks. He addresses God the Father, offers Jesus Christ to him, and prays in Jesus' name. But this is also your sacrifice; so get moving, make those words your own. Pronounce them in your heart. Read them in the missal or missalette if you do not know them by heart (or even if you do).

At the moment of the elevations make an act of faith, using the words of the apostle Saint Thomas: "My Lord and my God!" And then the Offering to the Merciful Love: "Holy Father, through the immaculate heart of Mary, I offer you Jesus, your most beloved Son, and in him, through him, and with him I offer myself for all his intentions and on behalf of all creatures." Realize that you truly are, at this moment, at the foot of the cross, witnessing Jesus' act of redeeming love. You are there; listen and speak to him, from deep within your heart.

6. *Communion*

Now you will want to do some final preparations, the last touches before receiving the divine guest. Say interiorly the prayer that the priest quietly recites: "Lord Jesus Christ, Son of the living God, by the will of the Father and the cooperation of the Holy Spirit your death brought life to the world. By your holy body and blood free me from all my sins and from every evil. Keep me faithful to your teaching, and never let me be parted from you."

While approaching the altar you can tell him in your heart, "I wish, my Lord, to receive you with the purity, humility, and devotion with which your most holy Mother received you. With the spirit and fervor of the saints."

Welcome him tenderly, and confide in him

with total trust and hope. For, as Father Eugene Boylan put it:

> . . . *It is as* our Savior *that* [*Jesus*] *enters into partnership with us. In fact, it is by that very partnership that he saves us. He comes to us full of perfect knowledge and unlimited love. He knows exactly what we are. . . . He knows all our defects and weaknesses. . . . He knows all that might have been done for us or by us, but which has been neglected. He knows all our mistakes and all our sins. . . . He knows all these things in advance, but being the perfect lover, he comes with the power of God to heal all these ills. He is perfectly prepared to repair our life completely if we do not prevent him. . . .*
>
> *Just as the two torn pieces of a sheet of paper fit perfectly together, so Christ fits perfectly into our life, and fills it completely. It does not matter how small is the part of the page which represents our life—or, if you prefer, our lack of life—he can and will supply all the rest of the page. He is our full complement; he is our perfect supplement. . . . In one Holy Communion we can receive the perfect complement of all our wasted past and our damaged self.* [24]

You know how, when you've taken your car to trusted mechanics to have one problem fixed, you will sometimes ask that, while they're at it, they check for and fix any other significant problems? Well, you might ask the Lord that, while he's there present within you, he go ahead and fix anything that's not to his liking. Give him carte blanche; you will not be sorry.

7. *Thanksgiving*

You have just been on Calvary, offering yourself with Jesus to the Father. The Sacrifice is over. Now you are in heaven. Jesus and you are one. This is a foretaste of eternal life. This is also Jesus' foretaste of life with you. As is the case with all lovers, what begins as a mutual embrace needs to become the starting point for confronting the world outside. After a while, the two of you should turn to face the world— your life today—together.

In the Mass, we stand before God the Father; we offer God the Son to him, and unite ourselves sacramentally to God the Son; and then we go our way, comforted by the continuous presence of God the Holy Spirit within us.

CONCLUSION

There are many other facets of the Holy Mass that I have not mentioned. Each in its own way helps us answer the question with which we started: *Why do we go to Mass?* When we are able to answer in all honesty, *Because I love it*, then our entire life revolves around it. The Holy Mass becomes "the center and the root of our spiritual life." [25] It becomes the point where all things in our life converge, and from where we draw all our spiritual strength.

I would like to share with you a little personal experience. One day, years ago, I got curious as to how long I could have Jesus within me in a lifetime of Holy Communions. So I did up some calculations. I knew this wasn't going to be an exact science, but the result took me by surprise.

It is the generally accepted understanding that the presence of Jesus in Communion lasts for about fifteen minutes—the approximate time it takes for our metabolism to destroy the sacramental species.

I myself began to receive Communion weekly at the age of seven, and daily at the age of fourteen. I thought, "Okay, suppose I live to be eighty-four." I found that if I died on my eighty-fourth birthday, I would have received our Lord 25,915 times. Multiplied by 15 minutes, that makes 388,725 minutes, or 6,479 hours, or 270 days. Which is the same as 9 months—the time that Mary had Jesus in her womb.

I repeat, this is only a rough calculation. In actuality, since I became a priest, I have often celebrated Mass and received Communion twice or even three times a day. And obviously none of us knows how long we are going to live in this world.

But there is no reason to feel jealous of Mary's intimate relationship with Jesus. Until we see him in heaven, there can be no greater intimacy than this.

I bring these meditations to a close with some words of the author of *The Lord of the Rings*. J. R. R. Tolkien was a daily communicant, a fact that puts him among those Catholics who go to Mass *because they love to*. Late in his life he wrote to one of his sons:

> *Out of the darkness of my life, so much frustrated, I put before you the one great thing to love on earth: the Blessed Sacrament. . . . There you will find romance, glory, honour, fidelity, and the true way of all your loves upon earth, and more than that: Death: by the divine paradox, that which ends life, and*

demands the surrender of all, and yet by the taste (or foretaste) of which alone can what you seek in your earthly relationships (love, faithfulness, joy) be maintained, or take on that complexion of reality, of eternal endurance, which every man's heart desires. [26]

❖

NOTES

1. Congregation of Rites, instruction, *Eucharisticum Mysterium*, no. 6. Quoted in *Catechism of the Catholic Church* (hereafter *Catechism*), no. 1325.

2. *Catechism*, no. 1366.

3. *Catechism*, no. 1364. Cf. Heb 7: 25–27.

4. See *Summa Theologica*, III, q. 46, a. 2 ad 3.

5. See *Catechism*, no. 1323. For that purpose God the Father also sent the Holy Spirit, one of whose roles is to "convince the world concerning sin" (Jn 16: 7). The sight of God's Son crucified alerts us *externally* to the gravity of sin, while the Spirit works *within* us, prompting us to acknowledge it. See Pope John Paul II, *Dominum et Vivificantem*, nos. 27–48.

6. I say "by himself" because he and the Son together have the Holy Spirit—who has also been given us.

7. *The Roman Missal: The Sacramentary* (New York: Catholic Book Publishing, 1974), p. 546. The translation is by the International Committee on English in the Liturgy, 1973.

8. Saint Josemaría Escrivá, *Christ Is Passing By* (New Rochelle, N.Y.: Scepter, 1982), no. 183.

9. *Catechism*, no. 1368.

10. Saint Ambrose, in *Preces selectæ* (Cologne: Adamas Verlag, 1987), p. 9.

11. Saint Augustine, *Confessions*, 9.11.

12. See Leo J. Trese, *Many Are One*, in *A Trilogy by Leo J. Trese* (Manila: Sinag-Tala Publishers, 1984), pp. 199–200.

13. *Christ Is Passing By*, no. 83.

14. Ronald Knox, *Retreat for Beginners* (Glen Rock, N.J.: Paulist Press, 1964), p. 116.

15. Excerpted from "Let the Son Shine Out," an article by Father Martin Lucia, first published in December 1995 (see http://www.cardinalkung-foundation.org). Bishop Sheen had already told this story in his autobiography, *Treasure in Clay* (Garden City, N.Y.: Doubleday, 1980), p. 120.

16. Saint Josemaría Escrivá, *The Way* (Princeton, N.J.: Scepter Publishers, 1992), no. 533.

17. *Retreat for Beginners*, p. 116.

18. See *Catechism*, no. 1401.

19. See *Catechism*, nos. 1850, 1855.

20. *Catechism*, nos. 1395, 1394 [cf. Council of Trent (1551): DS 1638], 1395 and 1415, respectively. The emphasis appears in the original.

21. Saint John Chrysostom, quoted in *Catechism*, no. 2179.

22. The texts quoted here belong to the *Order of Mass with a Congregation*. They are taken from *Handbook of Prayers* (Scepter Publishers and Midwest Theological Forum: Princeton and Chicago, 2001).

23. Saint Josemaría Escrivá, *The Way of the Cross* (New York: Scepter, 1983), Station VII, 3.

24. M. Eugene Boylan, O.Cist., *This Tremendous Lover* (Westminster, Md.: Newman Press, 1959), pp. 53–54.

25. Saint Josemaría Escrivá, Letter, 28 March 1955, no. 5.

26. Letter to Michael Tolkien, 6–8 March 1941, in *The Letters of J. R. R. Tolkien*, ed. Humphrey Carpenter (Boston: Houghton-Mifflin, 1981), pp. 53–54.